A GUIDE TO COOLE PARK

A photograph of Lady Gregory taken on the front lawn of Coole.

A GUIDE TO
COOLE PARK
CO. GALWAY

Home of Lady Gregory

BY

COLIN SMYTHE

WITH A FOREWORD BY

ANNE GREGORY

First published in 1973 by Colin Smythe Limited, Gerrards Cross, Buckinghamshire
Second edition, revised and enlarged, 1983
Third edition, revised, 1995

British Library Cataloguing in Publication Data
Smythe, Colin
A guide to Coole Park, Co. Galway. — 3rd rev. ed.
1. Coole Park (Co.Galway)
I. Title
914.17′4   DA995.G/

ISBN 0-86140-382-7

ACKNOWLEDGMENTS

My thanks to Macmillan, London, Limited, for permission to publish extracts
from *Collected Poems* of W.B.Yeats and to Michael B.Yeats and to Anne Yeats for
permission to reproduce illustrations by W.B.Yeats, Jack B.Yeats and John
B.Yeats, as well as the quotations from the poems. The lines beginning 'The
loud years come' on p. 68 are copyright © 1983 by Michael B.Yeats and Anne
Yeats.

The poems by John Masefield on p. 51 are copyright © 1983 The Trustees of
the Estate of John Masefield. The extracts from *Innishfallen Fare Thee Well* by
Sean O'Casey are published by permission of Macmillan, London, Limited.

Finally my deep indebtedness to the late Major R.G. Gregory, and to Mrs.
R. de Winton and Mrs. R. Kennedy whose recollections have helped to create a
living image of Coole for me and show me what it was like to live there. My
thanks too for so much more.

Produced in Great Britain
Typeset by Inforum Ltd, Portsmouth
and printed and bound by
T J Press (Padstow) Ltd, Padstow

FOREWORD

Coole Park was the headquarters of the Irish Literary Revival – no other place has a better claim to that distinction – but because I was born there and lived there continuously (apart from some school-ing in England), Coole still seems one thing only to me: home. During our childhood years, we – I, my brother Richard and my sister Catherine (known as Nu, as readers of *Me & Nu* will remember) – were looked after and cherished by our grand-mother, Lady Gregory. How she found time to do this in the midst of all her other activities I cannot imagine: she was writing plays and books, dealing with Abbey Theatre matters, and end-less correspondence over the Lane Bequest of French impression-ist pictures. This was quite apart from her involvement with jam-making, looking after her beloved young plantations and other home matters which would have been more than enough to fill anyone else's day, but she never appeared to have anything to do when we wanted her help or attention.

Sometimes there were visitors staying at Coole; W.B. Yeats of course, and Augustus John, and G.B.S. and Sean O'Casey . . . but we were young and did not realise that these were famous men. Yeats wrote that 'they came like swallows and like swallows went', but we children were really much more interested in the comings and goings of the real swallows.

After all these years I can still vividly remember nearly every step of the woods – the Nut Wood and Beech Wood especially – and of the Flower Garden. Of course there have been changes in both, but much of the magic still remains, and I get caught up in the wonderful, if nostalgic, memories of the place. The Flower Garden, though denuded of the majestic trees that were in one corner, the Irish yews standing like sentinels behind the vineries, and the great clump of enormous ilexes alongside the Autograph Tree (thankfully very much alive) still retains so much of the old days. For instance, the magnificent stone wall running from the entrance gate to the gate into the Nut Wood at the far end, and the box hedge in front of the long border remain nostalgically as before, and though generations of wall-flowers planted in the crevices of the wall have vanished, there are still some clumps of poet's laurel, of which Grandmama was always very proud.

But the woods, in spite of the loss of mature trees and the laying of modern pathways, still bring back all the happiness of my childhood, and I look twice at the stone seat under the great fir tree, almost expecting to see Grandmama sitting there, as she did so very often in the past.

I am continually amazed at the clarity of my memories of Coole after so very many years. I can shut my eyes and see myself and Nu in every part. Recently I worked out the floor plan of the house, something I have been meaning to do for years, but until this year, when I was able to sit down, with Colin Smythe encouraging me and my son drawing in the rooms as I described them, I was not able to concentrate long enough to work out how everything fitted together. I am so glad that the plans in this second edition of the *Guide* prove my success, with the final pieces in the jigsaw provided by my sister.

About ten years ago I returned to Coole for the first time in many, many years with reluctance and in some trepidation, fearing that I would be saddened by the changes. I wondered how I would react to seeing the ruins of the house and to everything done to make the estate more of an attraction to the many visitors who now come to Coole. But I need not have worried. I have been back a number of times since then, and I am happier to go back on each occasion. On my most recent visit I went round the Nut Wood, and felt that the peace of Coole was still there; and I looked back several times at the stone seat.

Anne Gregory

CONTENTS

ILLUSTRATIONS

CONTENTS

9

Above: the entrance avenue of ilex trees. *Below:* Coole woods. Photos by Gabriel Fallon.

COOLE PARK

I

TODAY

One and a half miles out of Gort on the Galway road, on the left hand side, you will see the entrance to Coole Park. Go along the drive for half a mile and you come to an avenue of ilex trees that form a gothic arch overhead. Passing under these, and following the road and signs, you will come to the foundations of a house. These are all that remain of Lady Gregory's home, Coole Park, the house that was the headquarters of the Irish Literary Revival. It was here that Lady Gregory wrote her books, plays and articles, and was host to W.B. Yeats, Douglas Hyde (founder and first President of the Gaelic League and later first President of Ireland), J.M. Synge, Bernard Shaw, George Russell (AE), Augustus John, her nephew Sir Hugh Lane, George Moore, John Masefield, Sean O'Casey, Jack B. Yeats, John B. Yeats, James Stephens, and a host of other figures, nearly all of whom produced works of lasting value while there, or perhaps as a result of their stay. That no stone of that historic house remains is the result of negligence, almost philistine indifference to the home of one of Ireland's greatest writers and patriots, one who chose to create rather than destroy, to build rather than pull down, but whose home was demolished in 1941 with the approval of the government of the time.

Although it can never be restored to its former state, after decades of neglect Coole has been transformed. Through the enthusiasm initially of the late Canon Grant Quinn, the Gort Archaeological Historical and Literary Society, the Department of Fisheries and Forestry and, most recently, the Office of Public Works with massive grants from the European Community, much has been done. The foundations of the house have been built up, the barn and stables converted into a Visitors' Centre that shows the history of the house and the geology, geography, flora and fauna of the region; there are car parks and many of the drives through the woods have been resurfaced; much of the land round the lake is a bird sanctuary; the flower garden with its famous copper beech has been transformed, and there are plans for further restoration.

To the left of the foundations, the road forks, the right-hand track leading to almost the only part of the estate that remained unchanged over the years, Coole Lake; of which Yeats wrote in 'The Wild Swans at Coole',

> The trees are in their autumn beauty,
> The woodland paths are dry,
> Under the October twilight the water
> Mirrors a still sky;
> Upon the brimming water among the stones
> Are nine and fifty swans.
>
> The nineteenth autumn has come upon me
> Since I first made my count;
> I saw, before I had well finished,
> All silently mount
> And scatter wheeling in great broken rings
> Upon their clamorous wings.

The left hand fork leads down to the stable-yard, and the Visitors' Centre. Anne Gregory remembers how it was:

The drive from the house down to the stables is completely bound up with childhood memories, and though of no great length – a hundred yards or so – it held much magic, particularly in summer, when the wonderful scent from the great lime trees and the deafening hum of the bees feeding from the lime flowers was intoxication enough.

Almost at once one came to the gate into the apple garden, full of gooseberries waiting to be eaten as they ripened, and of course a wondrous variety of apples. Below the garden gate was the door into the enormous barn, one third of which housed many tons of hay, while the rest was a wonderful squash court for use on wet days ... And then, at the end of the drive was the great cobbled yard. A very high wall at the back had a gate leading through into a part of the haggard, with piggeries, and calf-houses, etc., the front of the yard being open to the front lawn, and the buildings, running the length of the yard, faced each other along the sides. The actual stables for the horses consisted of eight loose-boxes on either side of a very large foaling box (which for many years housed the bust of Maecenas – or Macaenas as Lady Gregory called him – before it was put back in the flower garden.

The swans on Coole Lake, a drawing from the cover of Vere Gregory's book, *The House of Gregory* (1943).

Over (pp. 14-15): a map of Coole from an 1878 Ordnance Survey map. Using Yeats's spellings, the seven woods are (1) Shanwalla (uncertain: possibly old ruin, from the Irish *seanbhalla*; or old road, as an old avenue to the house ran through it); (2) Kyle Dortha (the dark wood); (3) Kyle-na-no (the nut wood); (4) Pairc-na-lee (the calves' field); (5) Pairc-na-carraig (rock field, also known locally as Fox Rock); Pairc-na-tarav (the bull field, the positioning of which is uncertain, but the grandchildren's memories place it here); (7) Inchy Wood (island wood, or water meadow wood). It is probable that the woods with fields in their names were originally fields planted with trees by the Nabob, Robert Gregory, or his descendants, before Lady Gregory lived at Coole. The names of the other fields round the house are: (8) the sawpit field; (9) the front lawn; (10) the back lawn; (11) the hobble field; (12) the stubble field; (13) the vegetable garden; (14) the flower garden; (15) the pond field.

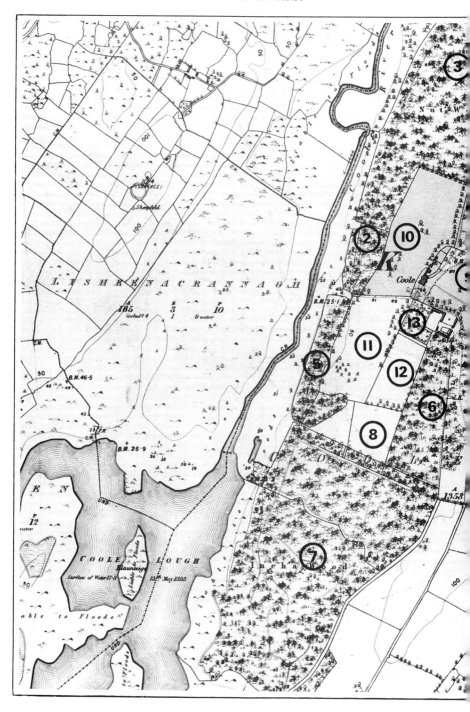

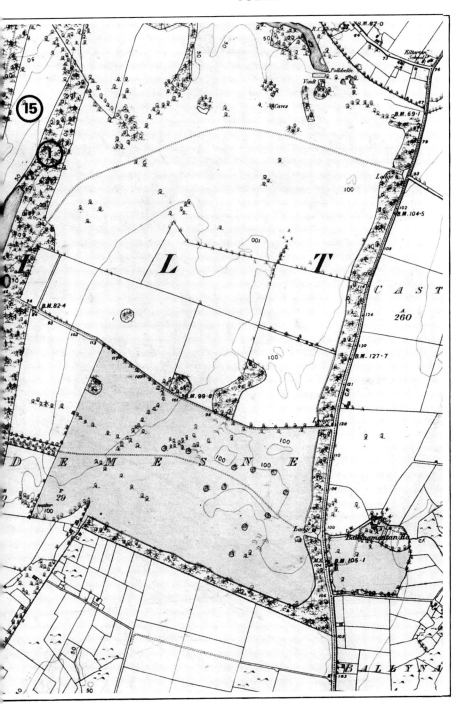

Opposite the stables were the large coach houses for all the various carriages and traps. There were five on each side of the harness room, and they all had immense arched double doors. They housed the two broughams, two side-cars, the Victoria, a dog-cart, a barricino (an Italian pony trap), the wagonette (which took all our luggage, food – vegetables, rabbits, chickens, etc. – and all the other impedimenta down to Burren for our summer stay at Mount Vernon), and finally the donkey trap, in which Grandmama used to drive round the woods, usually on her own, sometimes with a guest. The harness room, a very large room with a fireplace, had a heavenly smell of leather and turf-smoke, and from it a staircase went up to the coachman's flat upstairs.

These buildings, built of magnificent blocks of cut grey limestone, were a most impressive sight. They looked so wonderfully solid and permanent that it is hard to accept their demise.

Before its temporary sojourn in the foaling box, the bust of Maecenas had first been in the house, until one day it was carried out (it took four men) and placed against the east wall of the flower garden, where Lady Gregory wrote of it:

The sun . . . shines with a special warmth as it seems on the colossal marble bust of Macaenas at the end of the flower bordered gravel walk. Kiltartan tradition says this image was carried across Europe on waggons drawn by oxen; but it likely the width of land between its birthplace and an Italian seaport is a truer measure of its journey; and I know not from what harbour in Ireland it was carried to its resting place here.

As you go back up the road with the site of the house on your left, look to your right at the woodland and carparks. Between you and the entrance drive was all parkland with a cricket pitch at its centre and beautiful mature trees round its edges. On a visit in May 1902 Jack B. Yeats sketched one of the cricket matches that took place there, and Bernard Shaw is alleged to have played there, in a most civilised manner, employing a member of Lady Gregory's staff to retrieve the ball for him when he was fielding, so he could return it to the wicket. The legendary W.G. Grace was a visitor too, but the local people contended that he came more for the out-of-season shooting than for cricket. For over forty years trees were allowed to grow in a haphazard manner all over the area, but it is much tidier now than when I first saw it over twenty years ago.

Above: Robert Gregory (*left*) with the men who carried the Bust of Maecenas to the flower garden. *Below:* a cricket match at Coole in 1905, sketched by Jack B. Yeats.

Above: a cartoon from Robert Gregory's scrapbook. Regrettably neither the artist nor the characters, if not fictitious, are identified. *Below:* the teams of a cricket match at Coole. Robert Gregory is fourth from the right in the back row. The bearded man seated in front of him is probably the famous cricketer, W.G. Grace.

Walking straight ahead you will see the entrance to the walled 'flower garden', as it was called. Go through this and you will see box hedges, and towering ahead of you in the distance, standing out from all the trees on either side, a great copper beech. Go straight along the path and you will come to it. This is the tree on which many of Lady Gregory's most important guests carved their names. Unfortunately so many sightseers added theirs that a tall iron paling had to be put round the tree by the Kiltartan Society to prevent further additions. The initials are still visible, but there are now so many unauthorised sets that it is impossible to know which date from Lady Gregory's lifetime and which are later. Even her own 'key' to the initials has numerous blanks and queries, but when I came across it, I was able to correct my errors and omissions in the first edition of this *Guide*. (Unfortunately, others have perpetuated my mistakes.) In about 1928 Lady Gregory wrote of the tree:

And on the great stem, smooth as parchment, of a copper beech whose branches sweep the ground as we come near the gate into the woods, many a friend who stayed here has carved the letters of his name. W.B.Y. of course, and Jack B.Y. with a graving of the little donkey he loves; and J.M. Synge, and Æ and An Craoibhin (Douglas Hyde) and John Masefield and Sean O'Casey and as it should be, a very large G.B.S.. And this A.J. was cut by Augustus John after his descent from the topmost boughs where he had left those letters also to astonish the birds of the air.

Lady Gregory also had trouble with people carving their names on the tree without her permission, for she continues:

But alas! once or twice country lads doing some work in the orchard, seeing these signatures, thought it natural to add their own, and these unknown to literature, may puzzle some future antiquarian. And once I was just in time to catch hold of the penknives of some schoolboys from the United States who with their friends were spending an afternoon with us. It may be that I was too rash; that some day in that wonder-country there may be signed by a President in the White House the letters of a name that I had disallowed. Have not even angels been entertained unaware?

Once the yews protected the vineries, which are now gone although their rear walls still mark the site. A mature catalpa tree is still there, but it is badly damaged. Catalpa leaves appeared in

Margaret Gregory's illustrations for Lady Gregory's play *The Golden Apple* (1916). New trees have been planted to continue the tradition, and the fir trees that filled the flower garden two decades ago have been removed; the grass and flower-beds are tended once more, giving the visitor an idea of how it once looked when Lady Gregory lived there. When she was aged sixty, Yeats wrote a poem about her and Coole Park, 'The New Faces' (though he delayed publishing it for ten years at her request):

> If you, that have grown old, were the first dead,
> Neither catalpa tree nor scented lime
> Should hear my living feet, nor would I tread
> Where we wrought that shall break the teeth of Time.
> Let the new faces play what tricks they will
> In the old rooms; night can outbalance day,
> Our shadows rove the garden gravel still,
> The living seem more shadowy than they.

Walking round the estate one is struck by the atmosphere of Coole Park and even now, although the house had gone, there is something that draws and holds one to the place. But for those who knew Coole as it was, I fear that only the lake has not lost its magic and its beauty.

Above left: Lady Gregory under the catalpa tree. A photograph taken in 1927. *Above right:* an illustration by Margaret Gregory (Robert's wife) for Lady Gregory's play *The Golden Apple*, showing the catalpa leaves in the background. *Below:* Roxborough House, Lady Gregory's birthplace and home until her marriage in 1880, seven miles north east of Coole. Now in ruins. Photo courtesy of Mr. Dudley Persse and Mrs. E.M. Persse.

Above: a photograph of the Prince of Wales, later King Edward VII, with his entourage, and some of the British rulers of India and Ceylon, taken in Calcutta on 6 January 1876. The Prince, who is wearing a topee, is seated in the centre, behind the table. On his right is Lord Northbrook, the Viceroy of India, and on his left, the Viceroy's daughter, Lady E. Baring, and on her left, the recently knighted Sir William Gregory, K.C.M.G. *Below left:* a miniature of Sir William *c.*1850. *Below right:* the portrait of Sir William used in the first edition of his autobiography.

II

LADY GREGORY AND COOLE PARK

Isabella Augusta Persse was born about seven miles from Coole at Roxborough House in 1852, the twelfth of sixteen children. This house was her home for all her unmarried life. She had met Sir William Gregory, P.C., K.C.M.G., on his return to Co. Galway after he had retired from his position as Governor of Ceylon. Her liking for literature at first caused him to leave her in his Will the choice of any six books from his library in Coole, but the next time he changed it the whole library was hers to use, for she was by then his wife.

Miss Augusta (as she liked to be known) Persse married Sir William, who was thirty-five years her senior, in 1880 and in the following year their only child, Robert, was born. Before and during her married life she wrote a number of articles and short stories, some of which survive. After Sir William died in 1892, leaving the estate under her management in trust for Robert until he became twenty-one, she set about editing his autobiography, and this was published in 1894, quickly going into a second edition. Four years later she published the correspondence of Sir William's grandfather, who had been Under Secretary for Ireland between 1812 and 1831, and after whom he had been named.

By the time this second book had been published, Lady Gregory had met W.B. Yeats and the idea of an Irish Literary Theatre had been born, out of a discussion at the Count de Basterot's house 'Doorus' near Kinvarra, and was being actively promoted. Lady Gregory got guarantees from her friends to cover the expenses of the first season, which took place the following year in 1899 when Yeats's play *The Countess Cathleen* and *The Heather Field* by Edward Martyn (who was also a neighbour of Lady Gregory and whose home Tillyra – or Tulira – Castle still stands) were performed in the Antient Concert Rooms in Dublin. Yeats's play caused a stir because it was considered by some to be

Above: Coole; the entrance front in 1887. *Below:* the west front.
Facing page. Above: the library. *Below:* the drawing room.

anti-Catholic and Martyn kept on wanting to back out; however, he was persuaded not to and at the end of the run he even paid all the expenses. Thus the Irish Literary Theatre was born. For the first three years their season was only a fortnight in length, but after that it was decided to get hold of a theatre and put on plays throughout the year. Through the help, financial as well as practical, of Yeat's friend Miss Annie E. Horniman (of the tea family) a building was acquired, together with the necessary Patent. This was the Abbey Theatre. The first directors were Yeats, Lady Gregory (the Patent holder) and J.M. Synge.

Now she started to write plays to balance those of Yeats, and they became very popular: during her life she wrote and translated over forty, most of which were first performed at the Abbey and were usually very successful. Her one act plays *Spreading the News*, *The Rising of the Moon*, *The Workhouse Ward* and *The Jackdaw* are among the most famous of this genre.

Lady Gregory spent a great deal of her time at the Abbey, concerned with its day-to-day running as well as general policy. On one occasion she attended a rehearsal with Jack Yeats who sketched the group in front of him. The silhouette with the large hat could well be Lady Gregory's. His sketchbooks record his visits to Coole, and include pictures of a tea party by the lake, and a relaxed J.M. Synge up a tree. He drew many sketches in albums, and Lady Gregory had many of his pictures on the walls of Coole.

In 1919 Lady Gregory even acted at the Abbey, in the title role of *Cathleen ni Houlihan*, which she and Yeats had written, though it appeared under his name alone, and only recently has her part in its writing become well-known. She was prevailed upon to pose for some pictures at the time of the performances.

Coole Park became the headquarters of the Irish Literary Revival: Yeats spent much of each year there, writing poetry and plays, but there were other guests as well as those whom she mentioned in the passage about the copper beech, quoted above. Not everyone was honoured by being allowed to carve their names. Guests at Coole included John B. Yeats, the poet's father, John Quinn the New York lawyer, George Moore, W.G. Grace, the Fay brothers and Sara Allgood (these last three are definitely on the tree), Edward Martyn, Pamela Colman ('Pixie')

Above: a sketch by Jack B.Yeats of an early rehearsal of the Irish National Dramatic Society. The lady with the hat could be Lady Gregory. *Below:* Lady Gregory as Cathleen ni Houlihan, taken after the only time that she performed on the Abbey stage, with Arthur Shields as Michael, on 19 March 1919. As she said of the title role of *Cathleen ni Houlihan*, which she and Yeats had written in 1902, 'what is wanted but a hag and a voice?'.

Sarofield at Tea at Coole

A watercolour sketch by Jack B. Yeats of a picnic tea at Coole, near the lake. *Left to right:* Sarsfield, Lady Margaret Sackville (whom Lady Gregory had considered as a possible wife for Robert), Robert, T.A. Harvey (Robert's tutor, later Bishop of Cashel), 'Cottie' (Mrs. Jack B.) Yeats. The next sketch in the notebook shows Sarsfield throwing his head back in shock, having been given some tea to drink, and got it up his nose.

Smith, Sir Hugh Lane, Lady Margaret Sackville, Elinor Monsell, Violet Martin ('Martin Ross' of Somerville & Ross), and Emily Lawless, to name but a few.

Lady Gregory's nephew, Sir Hugh Lane, was Director of the National Gallery of Ireland at the time of his untimely death in the sinking of the *Lusitania* by a U-boat in 1915. In the unwitnessed codicil to his will he appointed Lady Gregory his trustee to see that his collection of thirty-nine French Impressionist pictures was returned to Dublin. Because the codicil was unwitnessed (although entirely in his handwriting), it was legally invalid, and Lady Gregory spent the rest of her life vainly trying to get the pictures

Lady Margaret   Robert   Harris   Cutler

back to Ireland. The details and history of her long struggle are given in her book on Sir Hugh Lane and in her *Journals*.

On 23 January 1918 Robert was killed while flying over North Italy with the Royal Flying Corps, shot down in error by a pilot of the Italian Air Force – Italy was Britain's ally in that war. This was a terrible blow to her, but neither she nor Yeats knew the details beyond the fact that he had been killed in action. Yeats wrote a number of poems about him and in that entitled 'In Memory of Major Robert Gregory' he summed up the dead man's abilities. Here are two verses (ix and x):

> We dreamed that a great painter had been born
> To cold Clare rock and Galway rock and thorn,
> To that stern colour and that delicate line
> That are our secret discipline
> Wherein the gazing heart doubles her might.
> Soldier, scholar, horseman, he,
> And yet he had the intensity
> To have published all to be a world's delight.

What other could so well have counselled us
In all lovely intricacies of a house
And blossoming garden path, or understood
All work in metal or in wood,
In moulded plaster or in carven stone?
Soldier, scholar, horseman, he,
And all he did done perfectly
As though he had but that one trade alone.

In Robert's standard service will he left all his property to his wife, although under Sir William's will Lady Gregory was allowed to live in the house for the rest of her life. She did her best to keep Coole for her grandson, Richard, who had been born and brought up there, as the 'heir male'. Robert's widow was more concerned with the hard financial facts of life, and the unsettled land situation caused her much worry, so eventually the estate was sold to the Government and after the sale Lady Gregory paid rent to it until her death in 1932.

She remained an active Director of the Abbey Theatre all her life and was vital to its continued existence, for on more than one occasion it was faced with collapse either because of disagreements with Dublin Castle who threatened to take away the Theatre's Patent, the riots over Synge's *Playboy*, or financial troubles, or the I.R.A.; or as once happened when Yeats was away and the manager Lennox Robinson was in the U.S.A. with the Abbey Company, Lady Gregory came up from Coole, and kept the theatre going with student actors until normality could be restored.

So this indomitable woman was, with Coole Park, the foundation, cornerstone and much of the superstructure of the Literary Revival in Ireland in the first quarter of this century. If she had not been there, with home and hospitality, and her determination to prepare for Home Rule and independence, Ireland's literary scene would have been very much poorer and the history of the country might have been very different.

Above left: Robert Gregory receiving the Légion d'Honneur. *Above right:* Robert's portrait of Arthur Sinclair as King James II in Lady Gregory's *The White Cockade*. Courtesy of the Abbey Theatre. *Below:* Another sketch by Jack B. Yeats, of Robert Gregory on Sarsfield at the Gort Show, 25 September 1906. Robert had performed the feats recorded in Yeats's poem 'In Memory of Major Robert Gregory' on Sarsfield and another, Kilcullen, which he had once ridden in the Galway point-to-point without reins or bridle, when the forehead strap of the bridle had broken.

The autograph tree (a copper beech) with a guide to some of the carved initials: (1) Theodore Spicer Simson; (2) Bernard Shaw; (3) Augustus John; (4) Douglas Hyde (An Craoibhin); (5) Lady Gregory; (6) Robert Gregory; (7) Violet Martin (real name of Martin Ross of Somerville and Ross); (8) G.W. Russell (AE); (9) W.B.Yeats; (10) Sean O'Casey; (11) Elinor Monsell; (12) J.M. Synge; (13) John Masefield, and two of those not on the photograph; (14) Jack B. Yeats; (15) Dame Ethel Smyth. Other signatures on the tree include Sara Allgood, Lennox Robinson, Lady Margaret Sackville, Frank Fay and William Fay, J.D. Innes, Robert Ross, General Sir Ian Hamilton, General Sir Neville Lyttelton, John Quinn the New York lawyer, and (16) the Countess of Cromartie.

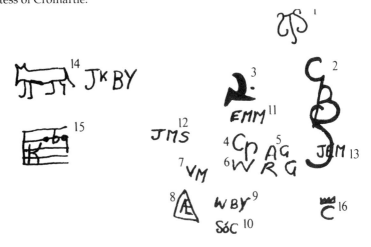

Above left: W.B.Yeats, Lady Gregory and a friend, seated in front of Coole. *Above right:* Bernard Shaw, a photograph taken on 16 April 1915 by the Rt. Hon. W.F.Bailey. *Below:* W.B.Yeats and George Moore outside Coole.

Above: Coole Lake, by Robert Gregory. Exhibited at the Chenil Gallery, London, in 1914, it was bought by Sir Hugh Lane, who left it to the Municipal Gallery in Dublin, which was recently renamed the Hugh Lane Municipal Gallery. *Below:* Belharbour by Robert Gregory. In a review in the *Observer* its critic reports on Robert's 'invariably well-arranged designs, which have a quiet charm of colour, in their restriction to slate grey, greyish purple and green, of which Mr. Gregory alone holds the secret. Even where he extends his palette to embrace more hopeful notes of blue, as in the delicious "Belharbour", the dominating feeling is still a dreamy sadness which is in absolute harmony with the barrenness and poverty of the soil.'

Above: one of Robert's theatre designs, the backdrop for J. M.Synge's *Deirdre of the Sorrows* (not Yeats's play *Deirdre*, as has been thought). Author's collection.
Below: the natural bridge at Coole, one of Robert's many paintings of the region. Sadly, the whereabouts of most of his pictures are unknown.

Above left: the portrait bust of the Rt. Hon. William Gregory, Under-Secretary for Ireland 1812–1831. *Above right:* the clay model of the statue of Sir William Gregory by Sir J.E. Boehm, which still stands in the Museum in Colombo, Sri Lanka. *Below:* Sir William, Lady Gregory and Robert in 1887, with two members of the staff. A photograph taken by Mrs. Ernest Hart.

III

THE HOUSE AND THE ESTATE

In 1768 Coole Park was purchased by a certain Robert Gregory (1727-1810), who had been born in Galway, gone to India where he had risen high in the Honourable East India Company's service and, by honest gain, became extremely rich. Although the estate was only about 600 acres, he later bought a dozen townlands, including over 1000 acres of the Ballylee estate from Lord Clanricarde, on which stood Thoor Ballylee, bought by W.B. Yeats in 1917. At the time of the sale of much of the estate in 1857, it consisted of over 15,000 acres.

In the same year that he bought Coole, Robert Gregory was elected M.P. for Maidstone, Kent, for which he sat until 1774, when he was elected for Rochester, in the same county. He was its M.P. until 1784. He was a Director of the East India Company from April 1768 till January 1783. In 1780 there was strong pressure for him to be made Governor of Madras, and in 1782 he became the company's chairman, but he had to resign at the end of July that year due to ill-health, 'occasioned by too close an application to business', as he put it.

At Coole, Robert Gregory had built a house and many miles of walls about the estate, most of which are still standing. Arthur Young visiting Coole Park in 1778, reported on his visit in *A Tour of Ireland* (1780):

September 4th to Kiltartan, the seat of Robert Gregory Esq. who is engaged in pursuits which, if well imitated, will improve the face of the country not a little. He has built a large house with numerous offices, and taken 5 or 600 acres of land into his own hands, which I found him improving with great spirit. Walling was his first object, of which he has executed many miles in the most perfect manner: his dry ones, 6 feet high, 3 feet and a half thick at bottom, and 20 inches at top, cost 2s.6d. the perch[5½ yards], running measure. Piers in mortar, with a gate and irons complete, £1.14s. Walls in mortar five feet high, cost 6s. a perch. He has fixed two English bailiffs on his farm, one for accounts and overlooking

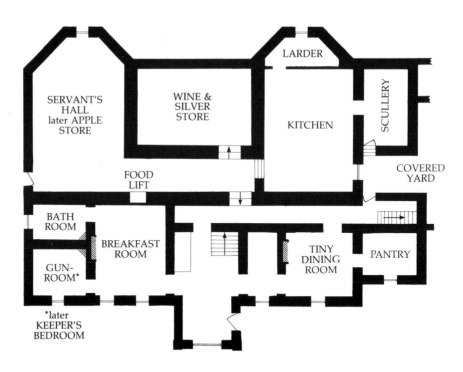

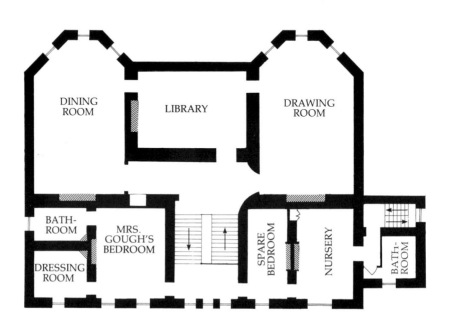

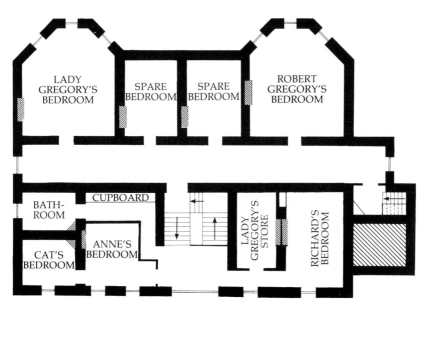

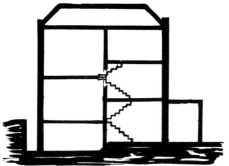

The interior of Coole. The house itself was on six levels, or more correctly six half-levels. On entering it by the front door, one went up half a floor to the main rooms, drawing room, library and dining room, below which were the kitchen, wine cellar, etc. that one reached by going down a few steps from the entrance hall. From the main level one climbed a further half flight to the nursery level, a half flight to the main bedroom level, above the library, and then a final half flight to the children's bedroom level. The two most important floors were therefore those looking west towards the Burren hills in the distance, on the opposite side to the entrance. They can be seen in the picture of the house on page 24, the kitchen level being completely obscured by the sloping ground. Yeats used one of the bedrooms above the library to work in. The front of the house was seventy-seven feet wide and the depth (including the nine foot bays), sixty-one feet.

his walling and other business; and another from Norfolk, for introducing the turnip husbandry, of which he has 12 acres this year: what particularly pleased me I saw some Irishmen hoeing them; the Norfolk man had taught them; and I was convinced in a moment that these people would by practice soon attain a sufficient degree of perfection in it. The soil around is a dry sound good limestone land, and lets for 10s. to 12s. an acre, some higher. It is in general applied to sheep. Mr. Gregory has a very noble nursery, from which he is making plantations, which will soon be a great ornament to the country.

After his death, successive generations continued to plant, down to Sir William, who scoured nurserymen's catalogues for rare trees to plant in his Pinetum, and Lady Gregory, who shared her husband's love for trees, and Robert. In an article on tree planting, published in *The Irish Homestead*, she wrote:

A little time ago my schoolboy son got hold of an axe, and cut down a tree – a deal one. But I told him that he must never cut one down without planting two in its place, so that very day he brought out an insignis and a silver fir from the nursery, and he planted them near a path that, if they thrive, he may see them all his life and remember their lesson.

Later in that article, she appealed to every Nationalist to plant at least one tree that year (1898), to every Unionist to plant one in 1900 and every waverer to plant one in the year in between.

Sean O'Casey said that her loves were books, which were nearest her mind, and trees, which were nearest her heart.

Unlike many of the surrounding big houses, Coole Park escaped destruction until after Lady Gregory's death; it remained empty, the property of the Government, until it was sold to a building contractor for the value of the stone. It had survived the Whiteboys of the 1870s, the Land Agitation, the Black and Tan and Auxiliary Troubles of 1919-20, and the Civil War of 1923. In 1910 Yeats wrote his poem 'Upon a House Shaken by the Land Agitation':

> How should the world be luckier if this house,
> Where the passion and precision have been one
> Time out of mind, became too ruinous
> To breed the lidless eye that loves the sun?
> And the sweet laughing eagle thoughts that grow

> Where wings have memory of wings, and all
> That comes of the best knit to the best? Although
> Mean roof-trees were the sturdier for its fall,
> How should their luck run high enough to reach
> The gifts that govern men, and after these
> To gradual Time's last gift, a written speech
> Wrought of high laughter, loveliness and ease?

And in another poem of the time, 'These are the Clouds', he wrote:

> The weak lay hand on what the strong has done,
> Till that be tumbled that was lifted high
> And discord follow upon unison,
> And all things at one common level lie.

As nothing now remains, here is a description of the house, taken from the late Edward Malins's foreword to the Dolmen Press edition (1971) of Lady Gregory's *Coole*:

One often finds an English or Irish country house stacked with pictures and furniture of the eighteenth or early nineteenth century, but with few examples of contemporary art. Coole was an obvious exception, its art ranging from Canova to Epstein, from Canaletto to Jack Yeats.

From her description one can see the walls of the Breakfast Room, lined with prints, engravings and lithographs – portraits of friends of the Gregory family since 1768 when they first came to Coole. There were statesmen such as Robert Peel and Lord Melbourne, or a fine engraving of Reynolds' portrait of Edmund Burke. Under this, the letter from Burke to his friend Robert Gregory who urged him to consider the natives as paramount in India: 'This was always your fundamental maxim: be assured it will be mine.' With what pride did Lady Gregory look at these prints, 'these memorials of high company' which Gregorys had brought home. And she knew that as a family, from Robert Gregory who had risen to be Director of the East India Company, to William his youngest son who was Under Secretary for Ireland, to his heir who died of famine fever while ministering to his tenants, to Sir William her husband, the Governor of Ceylon, they had a sense of service and a liberal turn of mind.

The house, which was built when Robert Gregory, the Nabob, purchased the estate, was rendered a yellowish-white tone over local stone; a slate roof, and neither grand nor imposing . . . In its setting of parkland . . . Coole did not give the feeling of having been built for defence as do many Irish eighteenth century houses, but rather as a dwelling where all were welcome. On the west side, the Victorian bow windows to the Drawing Room and Dining Room looked down to the lake, and even in the 1920s, after the trees had grown, the waters could be seen from the house. In fact, the view westwards toward the setting sun over the Burren, with the blue-shadowed Connemara hills in the distance was most beautiful as one approached along a wide drive through undulating parkland, before entering the gloom of the arched avenue of ilexes and limes.

Yeats was obviously struck by that beauty for he made a comment about it to John Masefield, later Britain's Poet Laureate, who described his own first visit to Coole in his *Memories of W.B. Yeats* (1940):

In the afternoons, I used to row him out onto the lake to fish (for perch and pike). When I first went there in the beauty of September, the lake was full. Under the burning sky, in the still shadows, the rocks of the lake had the greyness and strangeness of mirage. As we drifted into the lower lake, nine white swans rose up and clanked away from us. 'I have always thought,' Yeats said, 'this is the most beautiful place in the world.'

Such a day it must have been that Yeats remembered when he wrote 'The Wild Swans at Coole' years later.

In 1931 he wrote of Lady Gregory in her old age and her library which had been such a great influence on his early life:

> Sound of a stick upon the floor, a sound
> From somebody that toils from chair to chair;
> Beloved books that famous hands have bound,
> Old marble heads, old pictures everywhere;
> Great rooms where travelled men and children found
> Content or joy.

In *Coole* (written in 1928) Lady Gregory described the library and its contents before the final sale had taken place and when she feared that she would be unable to live there much longer. The possibility of blindness and senility also made her fearful:

I shall be sorry to leave all these volumes among which I have lived. They have felt the pressure of my fingers. They have been my friends.

Two pictures of Bernard Shaw at Coole, taken by the Rt Hon. W.F.Bailey in April 1915. *Above*: by Coole Lake. *Below*: with Lady Gregory on 16 April. Anne and Catherine are at the top right window, and Richard is at the wheel of the vehicle.

Above: cows by Coole Lake, taken by Bernard Shaw. *Below:* Lady Gregory near the natural bridge, taken by Mrs. Hart in 1887.

Now that the house is gone we can only walk round the estate, and try and look at it through Lady Gregory's eyes. In *Me & Nu: Childhood at Coole*, her grand-daughter Anne wrote:

Grandmama adored the woods, and taught us such a lot about them. Every year she planted a lot of young saplings, and endlessly walked round looking at her young plantations, tearing ivy away from the older ones, and seeing that the wire netting was safely around the smaller ones to keep the rabbits away. The weather had to be very bad indeed to keep her away from visiting at least the nearest seedlings. She always wore galoshes over her shoes, cotton gardening gloves over her mittens, and armed with her spud went forth daily to wage war against thistle, ivy, nettles, convolvulus and rabbits. I think one of the few times I saw her really furiously angry was when she found that several of her beautiful young larches had been cut down and taken away.

These larch trees were the subject of one of her poems, entitled 'The Forester's Year Book'.

Ten tender larch trees turned out in line:
Wicket wond wither; worries wan nine.

Brown bunny browsing barred out too late;
Brown bark delurable, delicate, on eight.

Harvest; hurry; bramble bush barring help of heaven;
Choked call of cripples, crying 'we are seven'.

Seven light leaders, clean candle-wicks;
Shy squirrel snuffs one, scampers scared from six.

Six sun-worshippers, sun-stirred sap of life;
Big beech bending broods over five.

Bare-branched-blight-grasped, bleeding at death's door;
Grey moss; mystery; whispered of by four.

Green greedy ivy grips growing tree;
Slack slasher striking saves only three.

Broad-branching barrier blots barren view;
Thinner's taste triumphs; breach between two.

Two scarred sentinels score setting sun;
Storm shrieks; west wind wails over one.

Tower-tall; rich-ringed; sixty years old:
Twenty-five shillings' worth, cross cut and sold.

Whenever she got a fee or royalty, she would first go out and plant another tree. If she received a particularly bad letter she would go out into the garden with her 'spud', a large stick with a sort of small chisel at the end, and poke up weeds, knock down thistles saying, 'So perish all the King's enemies'.

When Sean O'Casey came to visit, she taught him to distinguish between the various trees. 'She marched along telling their names, the way an eager young nun would tell her beads.'

And where is that glade that Sean described in the woods?

Occasionally, through the lusty leafage of hazel and ash, they caught a silver glimpse of Coole river flowing by, a river that bubbled up suddenly from the earth in a glade, a lonely corner, alive and gay and luminous with a host of pinkish-blue and deeply-blue and proud forget-me-nots; a secret corner that Lady Gregory had challenged Sean to find, and which had suddenly surrounded him on his third day of searching; a place so lovely in its blossoming loneliness that he felt he should not be there. Not a note from a bird disturbed its quietness; no lover and his lass, even, had passed through this glade; no breeze brought the faint lowing of far-off cattle to his ears; the blue of a serene sky overhead mantling the blue of the flowers at his feet; no sound save the musical gurgling whisper of the water calmly gushing out of the earth; so still, so quiet, so breathless, that Sean thought God Himself might well ponder here in perfect peace; and the merry Mab, in her mimic wagon, might journey home there through the tangled forest of forget-me-nots, without disturbing thoughts of things remembered in tranquility.

Yeats immortalised the woods in his poem 'In the Seven Woods'.

> I have heard the pigeons of the Seven Woods
> Make their faint thunder, and the garden bees
> Hum in the lime tree flowers; and put away
> The unavailing outcries and the old bitterness
> That empty the heart . . .
> I am contented, for I know that Quiet
> Wanders laughing and eating her wild heart
> Among pigeons and bees . . .

The bees were well-remembered by John Masefield when he sent Lady Gregory a letter in which he parodied one of her translations from the Irish:

Above: an envelope to John Masefield, embellished by its sender, Jack B. Yeats. *Below:* four lines that Yeats wrote in one of the special vellum bound copies of *The Wind Among the Reeds*, which he inscribed to Lady Gregory on April 14 1899.

Left: the front cover of Yeats's *The Tower* (1928) with the design by T. Sturge Moore, who has changed the position of the Tower in relation to the bridge to improve his design.
Below: Thoor Ballylee, by Robert Gregory. In the possession of Michael Yeats. Other versions of the picture exist.

Above left: a sketch of W.B. Yeats by his father John Butler Yeats, in Lady Gregory's copy of Lionel Johnson's *Ireland with other Poems*, drawn in September 1903. *Above right*: a sketch of W.B. Yeats by Lady Gregory, dated July 18 (no year). *Below left*: W.B. Yeats standing at the top of the steps in front of Coole with the front lawn, site of the cricket matches, behind him. *Below right*: W.B. Yeats in Rapallo, sporting a very temporary moustache and beard.

Above: Lady Gregory's bookplate with a pun on her maiden name, *Per Se* for Persse, to mean, as she told her grandchildren, that she herself designed and drew the bookplate.

Left: Robert Gregory's bookplate, printed by the Cuala Press. Later the design was to appear on the proof of the title page of the Cuala edition of Lady Gregory's *Kiltartan Poetry Book* (1918), but it did not look well, and was replaced in the published edition by his bell, fish and waterfall design first used in her *Book of Saints and Wonders* (1906).

It's pain in my heart to me that I was not born Irish
With a sweet tongue in my head and a pleasant way with me
For it's then I could have written the fine songs for Mr. Yeats, the great
   poet, and for Lady Gregory,
And written them strong and comely in a warm speech like the dear
   noise of the bees.

And after the gift of a copy of Lady Gregory's *Gods and Fighting
Men* on its publication in 1904, he launched into a similar poem:

It's my grief I am not a shepherd of the hills.
In blue cloak, lying among the fern, the sheep cropping at the grass.
With the wind blowing keen and steady, the wind full of sighs, full of
   songs, full of beautiful folk.
And I there, lying lonely, watching the great town and the sea.
For it's great wool my sheep would have, eating the pleasant grass with no
   ivy near.
It would be warm wool, white wool, wool for a queen, wool for a king,
   for a golden poet, for a woman that is the beauty of the world. It
   would bring me gold, and white silver, those pleasant fleeces,
The way I could buy all Lady Gregory's books, and the books of Mr.
   Yeats, and do nothing but read them till the day I died.

In a book of 'Mr Yeats' that he may have already read, *The Shadowy
Waters*, published in 1900 and dedicated to Lady Gregory, Yeats
had already named the woods in his prefatory poem:

> I walked among the seven woods of Coole;
> Shan-walla, where a willow-bordered pond
> Gathers the wild duck from the winter dawn;
> Shady Kyle-dortha; sunnier Kyle-na-no,
> Where many hundred squirrels are as happy
> As though they had been hidden by green boughs
> Where old age cannot find them; Pairc-na-lee,
> Where hazel and ash and privet blind the paths;
> Dim Pairc-na-carraig, where the wild bees fling
> Their sudden fragrances on the green air;
> Dim Pairc-na-tarav, where enchanted eyes
> Have seen immortal, mild, proud shadows walk;
> Dim Inchy wood, that hides badger and fox
> And marten-cat, and borders that old wood
> Wise Biddy Early called the wicked wood;
> Seven odours, seven murmurs, seven woods.

Above left: Lady Gregory by J.B. Yeats, dated June 3, 1903. In the possession of Sligo County Museum. *Above right:* John Quinn and W.B. Yeats in 1914, by Arnold Genthe. *Below left:* Sir Hugh Lane. *Below right:* Sean O'Casey, a photograph which he had inscribed for Lady Gregory.

Above left: Douglas Hyde by J.B. Yeats, which he had drawn in Lionel Johnson's *Ireland and other Poems* at the same time as the portrait of W.B. Yeats on p.49. *Above right:* J.M. Synge, by Robert Gregory, originally reproduced in Lady Gregory's *Our Irish Theatre*, and now in the possession of the National Gallery of Ireland. *Below left:* a quick self-portrait sketch that G.W. Russell (AE) did in one of Lady Gregory's scrapbooks. *Below right:* a self-portrait, dated 1921, by J.B. Yeats now in the possession of the Sligo County Museum.

Above left: Robert Gregory in June 1902, one of a number of photographs taken to mark his coming of age. *Above right*: Robert in flying kit. *Below left*: Robert's wife, Margaret, with Richard in 1909 at Coole, and *below right*, their three children, c.1916, in ascending size (and age), Catherine ('Nu'), Anne and Richard, called 'the chicks' by Lady Gregory in her *Journals*.

During Lady Gregory's walks she would often see wood-cock and, more rarely, pheasant, as well as snipe, teal and wild duck, and of course the swans, on the lake or winging overhead.

Four-footed creatures also make themselves at home in the woods. Even at no great distance from the garden gate I have seen a fox pacing slowly, silently, in the centre of one of the green walks; turning his head right and left, listening also no doubt with those pricked ears for the rustling of a rabbit moving in the grass, or more mischeviously nibbling bark from the young tree stems. In Pairc-na-Carraig the rock wood, a badger once crossed Yeats' path so close, so absorbed in its quest, that he touched with his hand its thick covering before it vanished in alarm. The children's dogs, less fortunate, came back a year ago from a night out, badly clawed and bitten after a fight as we believe with one or more of these. They had suffered at another time, attacking a fox, poor wretch, coming from fields not ours with a trap hanging to its pad, though they brought its torment to an end.

The squirrels, my enemies for all their innocent looks, because of their ill-treatment of the bark of my young trees, do not use their sharp teeth upon flesh and blood. Poor old Tonks, an Irish Terrier, had all through his life the ambition to kill one and would stand barking and clawing at a tree up whose trunk one of them had clambered, and it may be sat teasing him with grimaces.

It is long since I have come across a hedgehog. I used often to see them in the untilled wildness of the park. They are fabled to be of use in a garden, destroying mice it may be or slugs, and once or twice I had one carried here, but never saw it again. Once we tried to bring up a very young one by hand – I have in my room a pastel by A.E. showing it and his little son Brian sitting face to face on the gravel before the Hall door. But it vanished I know not where. It was not old enough to 'stick an apple on every thorn, and away with it to a scalp with them, to be eating through the winter' as I have heard is one of their habits. I have been told also of one, a 'granoge' as is the country name, met by the teller of the tale on the mountain. 'And, that I may never sin, he was running up the side of it as fast as a racehorse.'

Weasels have a bad name with our gamekeepers although a kindly neighbour says: 'The poor creatures, they will touch nothing at all on you if you behave well to them and let them alone. But if you do not they will not leave a chicken in the yard.' And 'to see a weasel passing the road before you, there's nothing in the world like that to bring you all sorts of good luck'. And once, on the Clare coast, a passer-by called out to me, and as I came to meet him said, 'I thought the tide might steal on you, or a weasel might chance to come up with a fish in his mouth and to give you a start. It's best if you see one to speak nice to it and to say 'I wouldn't be begrudging you a pair of boots or of shoes if I had them'.' But so far in my life I have never come near enough to a living weasel to make this insincere offer of a liberal friendship. Nor did I need the advice of another old acquaintance not to 'insult one; for if you pelt them or shoot them they will watch for you for ever to ruin you. For they are enchanted and understand all things.'

The marten cat is no longer I think an inhabitant of our woods. Yet a score or so of years ago its beautiful fur, hardly to be known from sable, made winter trimmings for our coats, so often were they found in the rabbit traps, or so the old Keeper said. But he hated them, believed they devoured the pheasants eggs, and I suspect it was his gun that ran up the score of pelts. One day hearing that a marten cat have been taken alive in a trap and brought into the stables, I went out to see it there, and well remember its eyes of green fire. It was but a toe that was held by the steel teeth, & I said it must be set free, though it was no loving look that had been turned on me by those blazing eyes. I had all the dogs locked up before the stable door was set open, and when the steel jaws were loosened the little beast made for the door like a flash and vanished into the nearest edge of the Shanwalla wood. A little later when the dogs were released they had not forgotten their disappointment, and were on the trail in a moment. But there was no chance for them, it had travelled maybe its hundred acres, (as our cats are said to do in the night time) in the treetops above our heads. But when some time later a marten cat was brought in dead, I sent it to a Dublin taxidermist for I felt sure, and was not mistaken, that the home here of these wildest creatures could not long be preserved; too many noises were coming near us in this twentieth Century, some better forgotten, the blowing up of bridges, the rattling of armoured cars. And later yet, that aeroplane lost in its flight over the Atlantic, passed so low over our lawns and woods, the last those hapless voyagers were ever to see, that the cattle ran terrified here and there, and it is likely the twitter of birds was silenced and all the wild creatures trembled, their race memory recalling no such regular throbbing in any thunderous storm.

Lady Gregory then describes the river which runs through the estate and tells the story of the birth of St. Colman, said to have taken place on its banks, and other strange happenings.

Our own river that we catch a glimpse of now and again through hazel and ash, or outshining the silver beech stems of Kyle Dortha, has ever

Lady Gregory's fans on which she collected signatures. *Above*: the earlier one; signatures on this include those of Sir John Millais, J.E. Boehm, James McNeill Whistler, Sir Alfred Lyall, Lord Tennyson, G.F. Watts, the Marquess of Dufferin & Ava, and Lord Randolph Churchill. On the other side are those of John Bright, Sir Edward Malet, Sir Arthur Sullivan, Wilfrid Scawen Blunt, Ahmed Arabi, W.E. Gladstone, A.W. Kinglake, Sir G.O. Trevelyan, and Sir Henry Layard. On the more recent one (*below*), there are signatures of, among others, Henry James, W.E.H. Lecky, J.A. Froude, Sir William Orpen, Bret Harte, Mark Twain (S.L. Clemens), Theodore Roosevelt, Thomas Hardy, Ramsay MacDonald, Ellen Terry, Robin Flower, Antonio Mancini, Finley Peter Dunne, Augustus John, H.H. Asquith, Rudyard Kipling, Bernard Shaw, J.M. Synge, George Moore, John Eglinton (W.K. Magee), Sean O'Casey, An Craoibhin Aoibhin (Douglas Hyde), Jack B. Yeats, AE (G.W. Russell), W.B. Yeats, Edward Martyn and James Stephens.

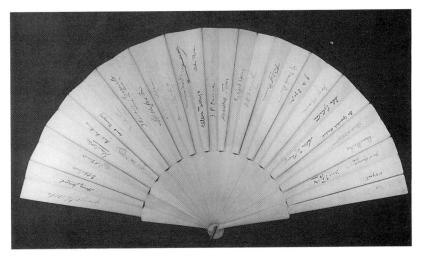

Two photographs by Bernard Shaw: Lady Gregory at her desk, and W.B. Yeats on the shore of Coole Lake.

Three men in a boat: W.B. Yeats, J.M. Synge and AE (G.W. Russell), fishing on Coole Lake. This was drawn by Harold Oakley, a friend of Robert, whom he had met at the Slade School of Art, where they both studied.

Above: Coole, a photograph taken by Bernard Shaw in 1915. *Below:* Coole, partly demolished, 1941. The Irish government had considered using it as a military hospital, but the local surveyors who looked over it considered that it was in such a state of neglect, after being empty for nine years, that the cost of making it habitable again would be too great to justify the expense.

been an idler. Its transit is as has been said of human life 'from a mystery through a mystery to a mystery'; suddenly appearing as a French writer has put down in his book 'dans le beau parc privé de Coole, derrière le village de Kiltartan'. And dipping presently under great limestone flags that form a natural bridge 'la dernière rèapparition se fair voir à 350 metres de là toujours dans le parc de Coole.' Then, flowing free, it helps to form a lake, whose fulness, finding no channel above ground is forced 'de chercher sa route par les passages souterrains de lac vers la mer'; into which it flows under the very shadow of the Dun of the ancient legendary King Guaire; he who having heard that a child to be born to a certain woman would be greater than his own son 'bade his people to make an end of her before the child would be born. And they took her and tied a heavy stone about her neck and threw her into the deep part of the river where it rises within Coole. But by the help of God, the stone that was put about her neck did not sink but went floating upon the water, and she came to the shore and was saved from drowning.' And the name of the child that was born, Saint Colman, is held in honour all over Ireland, and it is told that he has done many kindnesses to the people of this place. 'There was a little lad in Kiltartan one time that a farmer used to be sending out to drive the birds off his crops, and there came a day that was very hot and he was tired and he dared not go in or fall asleep, for he was in dread of the farmer beating him. And he prayed to Saint Colman, and the Saint came and called the birds into a barn, and they all stopped there through the heat of the day till the little lad got a rest, and never came near the grain or meddled with it at all.'

(Yeats referred to the river in his poem 'Coole Park and Ballylee, 1931':

> The waters that rise in a rocky place
> In Coole Demesne, and there to finish up
> Spread to a lake and drop into a hole.
> What's water but the generated soul?

He thought that the river passing by his Tower was the same as Coole river, but geologically it cannot be.)

Folk-lore has continued to gather around this place and a far later story has been told me of two men who 'went into a field near to where the river rises, one night to catch rabbits. And when they were standing there they heard a churning. So they went on a little way and they heard a tambourine below, music going on and the beating of a drum. So they moved a little farther and they they heard the sound of a fiddle from below. So they came home and caught no rabbits that night.' And a girl who 'had brought the dinner to two men working there, and began to gather kippeens [fircones, small sticks] and put them in her shawl, and to twist a rope of the ends of it to tie them up, was taken up, and where she found herself was in Galway sitting in the Square.' And once 'A great blast of wind came and the trees were bent and broken and fell into the river and the splash of the water out of it went up to the skies. And those that were with us saw many figures, but myself I only saw one, sitting there by the bank where the trees fell. Dark clothes he had, and he was headless.'

But anglers are in no dread of such appearances, and many a fine trout has been landed on the grass and bracken of the banks.

And the river, passing under a natural bridge formed of great limestone flagstones again sinks, again rises, then joining with another stream flows on till we see it shining through the spreading beech trees of Kyle Dortha, a wood destroyed, tradition says by some calamity of burning that is not kept so clearly in the mind of the people as 'the Big wind' of 1847. And a later storm, of 1903 was troublesome enough to me, and comes sadly to mind as I pass by those acres of Pairc-na-Carraig where thousands of tall conifers were otherthrown by the fierce wind that cuts its wide path through our demense. That news had come to me one evening in London, the very evening as I well remember when friends, Yeats and Arthur Symons and Florence Farr, I forget if there were two or three others – had come to dine with me. I was about to read to them Synge's new play, but seeing a home letter and taking it to read in another room with no ill presentiment, line after line told of some new disaster – nine great limes felled between house and stable yard; our demesne walls broken by falling trees, the public roads blocked; the great ilex on the lawn under which men and boys used to gather to watch our cricket matches (in which we had never been beaten until after its fall). I said nothing to my guests, and the play being *Riders To The Sea* its tragedy suited my mood.

And I think it was these Coole woods and not those of Alban that were in Synge's mind later when he wrote, 'Who'll pity Deirdre has lost the twilight in the woods with Naisi, when beech trees were silver and copper, and ash trees were fine gold.' For when staying here he never went out upon the roads, these sylvan walks were his delight.

Going out from the garden to that path by which one sees the rare foreign conifers planted by my husband and that are now great towering pyramids, I come to and look upon with pride, some acres of my own planting that with less of strangeness have in their planter's eyes an equal beauty in the white stems of silver fir, the rosy blossoms, the

Above: Doorus, the Count de Basterot's home, at which the idea of the Irish Literary Theatre was born in 1897. In his time, it was spelled Duras. *Below*: Tullira (Tillyra) Castle, Edward Martyn's home.

Above: Corley the Piper, with W.B. Yeats, Lady Gregory, and possibly Robert, outside Coole. *Below*: a sketch by Jack B. Yeats of J.M. Synge relaxing in the branches of a tree at Coole in 1905.

Lady Gregory, by Antonio Mancini, a portrait done at the same time as the famous one in the National Gallery of Ireland. It passed through Christies in 1949, and is now somewhere in Italy.

delicate green branches of the larch. Many an hour I have spent among them – for in a nursery of trees, as of children, one may run the whole gamut of joy and anxiety, of pride and of fear – my companion and best helper an old man, now passed away. Many a time in winter snow we have gone out together with tar and brush to make the bark distasteful to hungry rabbits, or in summer time, he with slasher, I with spud, to free our nurselings from the choking of bramble or of grass. He was an old master of the business, had loved it through his lifetime. And as an English statesman Arthur Balfour said and found true of a friend of mine [AE], 'I have never known a mystic who was not practical', so John Farrell, working as he spoke, Yeats sometimes a listener, would tell me of strange visions. 'I was cutting trees over in Inchy one time, and at eight o'clock one morning when I got there I saw a girl picking nuts, with her hair hanging down over her shoulders, brown hair. And she had a good clean face and was tall, and nothing on her head, and her dress was no way gaudy but simple. And when she felt me coming she gathered herself up and was gone as if the earth had swallowed her. And I followed her but I never could see her again from that day to this, never again.'

There are many tales of strange appearance in Inchy, that wild unplanted wood – some cedars there were believed to have come from seed dropped by birds that had travelled home from the Holy Land. It lies beyond the rock cavern where the water of the lake disappears from us, on its hidden journey to the sea. The water that had known unearthly visitors, heard unearthly sounds at its rising, is not without them as it vanishes from our sight. And it was not old Farrell but another who told me that his grandfather 'watching there one night where the lads from Gort used to be stealing rods, was sitting by the wall, and the dog beside him. And he heard something come running from Inchy weir, and he could see nothing, but the sound was like the sound of the feet of a deer. And when it passed by him the dog got between him and the wall and scratched at it, but still he could see nothing but only could hear the sound of hoofs. So when it was passed he turned away home.'

It was over at Inchy weir also, beyond that field of rocks covered by spreading juniper, that as a man still living told me, he and his brother had gone one day in their boyhood to catch a horse. 'And growing close by the water there was a bush the form of an umbrella, very close and thick at the top. So we began fooling as boys do, and I said, 'I'll bet a button none of you will make a stone go through that bush'. So I took up a pebble of cowdung and threw it, and they all threw, and no sooner did the pebble hit the bush than there came from it music like a band playing. So we all ran for our lives and when we had got about two hundred yards we looked back and we saw something moving round the bush, first it had the clothes of a woman and then of a man.' And he told also of a tragedy in later years, the blinding of a boy by a thorn as he, ignorant of danger and working under orders, had attempted to cut down that bush. And there also, by Inchy gate, there was a journey from a wedding 'at dead of night. And all of a minute the road was filled with men and horses riding along, and the horsemen calling out the name of a man who had been married that day. And twenty-one days after, that man lay dead. There's no doubt there were no riders belonging to this world that were on those horses.'

And another told me, 'One day I was coming home from Tirneeven School, and as we passed Dhulough that is beside Inchy, we heard a great splashing and we saw some creature put up its head with a head and a mane like a horse. And we didn't stop but ran. But I think it was not so big as the monster over here in Coole Lake, for Johnny Callan that saw it said it was the size of a stack of turf. But there's many could tell about that, for there's many saw it.' And another old inhabitant had been out on the lake with two or three men, 'and one of them had an eel spear and he thrust it into the water, and it hit something and the man fainted, and they had to carry him in out of the boat to land. And when he came to himself he said that what he struck was like a horse or like a calf, but whatever it was it was not a fish.' But a less terrible vision was told of by another who 'saw two ladies down by the lake, and I thought it was the ladies from the house gone out for a walk. But when I came near it was two strange women I saw sitting there by the lake, and their wings came and they vanished into the air.'

Even if one is only on a short visit to the west of Ireland, one cannot help being aware, particularly when alone, of the proximity of the supernatural to the natural normal ways of our daily life. Lady Gregory collected the stories and experiences of the people of the region over a period of twenty years of more, and published the collection as *Visions and Beliefs in the West of Ireland* which describes the folk-lore, healing herbs, charms, strange visions, seers and healers, the forths and the sheoguey (faery) places of Connaught.

Perhaps Coole Park's finest hour was when Lady Gregory was its mistress, when great men, in Yeats's words,

> . . . came like swallows and like swallows went,
> And yet a woman's powerful character
> Could keep a swallow to its first intent;

And half a dozen in formation there,
That seemed to whirl upon a compass point,
Found certainly upon the dreaming air,
The intellectual sweetness of those lines,
That can cross time and cut it withershins.

(In his Rapallo Diary, he describes the genesis of this poem. 'Coole Park, 1929', thus:

'Describe house in first stanza. Describe Lady Gregory. Here Synge came, Hugh Lane, Shawe-Taylor – many names – I too in my timid youth – Coming and going like the migratory birds. Then address the swallows fluttering in their dreamlike circles. Speak of the rarity of the circumstances that bring together such concord of men. Each man more than himself, through whom an unknown life speaks. A circle, love turning unto itself.)

In a vellum bound copy of *The Wind Among the Reeds* that Yeats inscribed to Lady Gregory on April 14 1899, he wrote the following lines that I do not think he ever used elsewhere:

The loud years come the loud years go,
A friend is the best thing here below;
Shall we a better marvel find
When the loud years have fallen behind?

Much has and will be written about the friendship of Yeats and Lady Gregory, out of which grew one of the greatest literary partnerships of the twentieth century, and the industry – academic and tourist – based on their work and on the work of the other members of the Literary Revival continues to grow, and seems an unstoppable tide.

For Coole, the end came with Lady Gregory's death. The house had become more and more difficult to maintain as costs and rates rose and her income did not. She had always tried to avoid being a burden on her daughter-in-law, Margaret, by paying for its expenses through her earnings as author and playwright, and had given up her income from Sir William's will in 1908 when the entail on the estate was broken, but the burden became impossible for them both, and in 1927 the house was sold, Lady Gregory subsequently renting the house from the Forestry Department of the Land Commission. (I am glad to say that the estate is now owned by the Office of Public Works, who have made it into an internationally recognised nature reserve.)

On Lady Gregory's death in 1932 the contents were auctioned, or put in store, the house remaining empty until it was sold and demolished in 1941-42. Yeats guessed its fate when he wrote in the last stanza of 'Coole Park, 1929':

> Here traveller, scholar, poet take your stand
> When all those rooms and passages are gone
> When nettles wave upon a shapeless mound
> And saplings root among the broken stone
> And dedicate – eyes bent upon the ground,
> Back turned upon the brightness of the sun
> And all the sensuality of the shade –
> A moment's memory to that laurelled head.

The portrait medallion of Lady Gregory by Theodore Spicer Simson. His lyre-like monogram is above Shaw's initials on the autograph tree.

INDEX

THE COOLE EDITION OF
LADY GREGORY'S WRITINGS

General editors: T. R. Henn and Colin Smythe

VISIONS AND BELIEFS IN THE WEST OF IRELAND
CUCHULAIN OF MUIRTHEMNE
GODS AND FIGHTING MEN
OUR IRISH THEATRE
COLLECTED PLAYS 1 COMEDIES
COLLECTED PLAYS 2 TRAGEDIES AND TRAGIC-COMEDIES
COLLECTED PLAYS 3 WONDER AND THE SUPERNATURAL
COLLECTED PLAYS 4 TRANSLATIONS, ADAPTATIONS AND
                              COLLABORATIONS
THE KILTARTAN BOOKS (POETRY, HISTORY AND WONDER)
SIR HUGH LANE: HIS LIFE AND LEGACY
POETS AND DREAMERS
A BOOK OF SAINTS AND WONDERS
SEVENTY YEARS
THE JOURNALS (2 VOLS)
THE LECTURES
SHORTER WRITINGS (2 VOLS)
THE AUTOBIOGRAPHY OF SIR WILLIAM GREGORY
MR. GREGORY'S LETTER BOX, 1813–35
GENERAL INDEX, BIBLIOGRAPHY AND LIST OF BOOKS IN COOLE
  LIBRARY